U.S. HISTORY TIMELINES

colonization
1607-1760

Megan Kopp

MEDIA ENHANCED BOOKS
AV2 BY WEIGL
ADDED VALUE • AUDIO VISUAL

www.av2books.com

AV² provides enriched content that supplements and complements this book. Weigl's AV² books strive to create inspired learning and engage young minds in a total learning experience.

Your AV² Media Enhanced books come alive with...

Audio
Listen to sections of the book read aloud.

Key Words
Study vocabulary, and complete a matching word activity.

Video
Watch informative video clips.

Quizzes
Test your knowledge.

Go to www.av2books.com, and enter this book's unique code.

BOOK CODE

U 1 9 0 3 5

Embedded Weblinks
Gain additional information for research.

Slide Show
View images and captions, and prepare a presentation.

AV² by Weigl brings you media enhanced books that support active learning.

Try This!
Complete activities and hands-on experiments.

... and much, much more!

Published by AV² by Weigl
350 5th Avenue, 59th Floor
New York, NY 10118
Websites: www.av2books.com   www.weigl.com

Library of Congress Cataloging–in–Publication Data available upon request.

ISBN 978–1–4896–0708–9 (hardcover)
ISBN 978–1–4896–0709–6 (softcover)
ISBN 978–1–4896–0710–2 (single–user eBook)
ISBN 978–1–4896–0711–9 (multi–user eBook)

Printed in the United States of America in North Mankato, Minnesota
1 2 3 4 5 6 7 8 9 0   18 17 16 15 14

052014
WEP301113

Project Coordinator: Aaron Carr
Editor: Pamela Dell
Designer: Mandy Christiansen

Every reasonable effort has been made to trace ownership and to obtain permission to reprint copyright material. The publishers would be pleased to have any errors or omissions brought to their attention so that they may be corrected in subsequent printings.

Weigl acknowledges Getty Images as its primary image supplier for this title.

CONTENTS

Settling a New Land

By the 1600s, the English were taking a serious interest in **colonizing** North America. The first attempt to start an English **colony** occurred in 1585 on Roanoke Island, off the shores of what is now North Carolina. For unknown reasons, that effort failed. The colonists and their **settlement** had disappeared by the time other settlers arrived.

It took another 20 years to establish the next English colony. That settlement began in 1607 on Jamestown Island in Virginia. The Jamestown colonists faced conflicts with American Indians. They endured severe food shortages and new diseases. Hard work and strong beliefs paid off, however. The colony survived. This success pushed England's efforts to colonize even further.

THE TRIANGULAR JAMESTOWN settlement had houses, a church, and storehouses for weapons and other supplies.

SHIPS AHOY!

Many ships had a role in populating the colonies in the early 1600s. The best known of these was the *Mayflower*. That ship first carried settlers to what is now New England in 1620. Earlier, in 1607, the *Susan Constant* was the largest of three passenger ships that brought settlers to Jamestown. In 1621, the *Fortune* delivered new arrivals to New Plymouth. The ships *Little James* and *Anne* carried colonists to New Plymouth in 1623.

POPULATION IN THE COLONIES

The Jamestown colony began with about 100 people. The population of the American colonies as a whole grew slowly in the early 1600s. At the same time, the American Indian population suffered many losses. In 1616, an outbreak of smallpox took the lives of thousands of American Indians in New England alone.

ENGLAND'S COLONIAL QUEST

North America offered the possibility of wealth and religious freedom. Many left Europe to settle in English colonies for these reasons. However, people that were interested in increasing England's territory and influence had another reason. They wanted to limit Spanish **expansion**.

FISHY BUSINESS

At first, colonists had few survival skills. Over time, however, settlers on the East Coast learned to fish with great success. By 1640, fishing was a major industry in New England. That year, the Massachusetts Bay colony traded 300,000 cod.

Jamestown

In 1606, England's King James I granted a **charter** to the Virginia Company. The company's goal was to establish a colony in North America and look for gold. The charter was the first step in setting up the Jamestown colony. On May 14, 1607, three ships carrying 104 Virginia Company colonists arrived in North America. The colonists settled in the Chesapeake Bay region, and they called it Jamestown. Jamestown, in what is now Virginia, was the first permanent English settlement in North America.

In September 1608, an explorer named John Smith became the colony's president. Under Smith's strict leadership, Jamestown began to succeed. This success was short-lived, however. Smith was injured in 1609 and returned to England. For the next seven years, the small colony struggled to survive. Then, in 1616, the settlers learned how to grow tobacco. This was the first step in securing Jamestown's future.

1585–1640   1606   1609–1629   1619–1650   1620–1621   1629–1650

1616

Smith was one of Jamestown's founders. An adventurer, he led trips inland to trade with American Indians for food such as corn. On one trip, Smith was captured by Powhatan Indians. Although there is no proof, an old legend claims Chief Powhatan's favorite daughter saved Smith's life. This young girl was named Pocahontas.

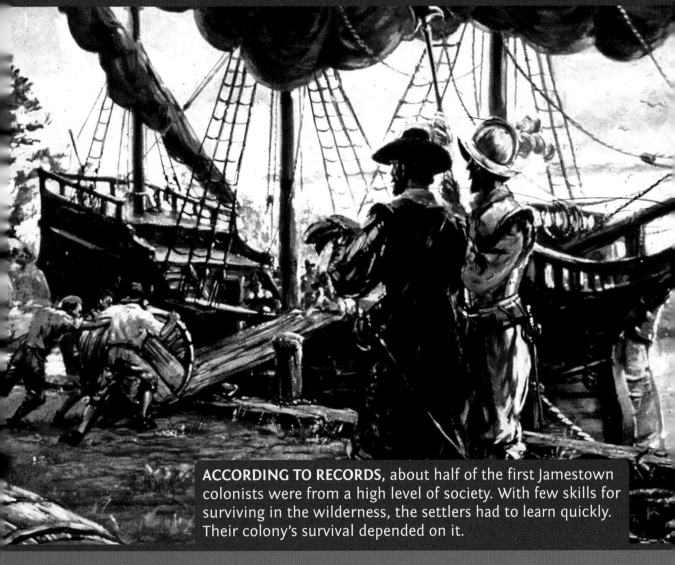

ACCORDING TO RECORDS, about half of the first Jamestown colonists were from a high level of society. With few skills for surviving in the wilderness, the settlers had to learn quickly. Their colony's survival depended on it.

Tobacco

The Jamestown colonists experimented with many different ways of making money. They created glassware. They harvested **timber** for sale and experimented with silk-making. None of these brought much **income**.

Then, in 1609, a settler named John Rolfe arrived in Jamestown with a few seeds from a tobacco plant. From these seeds, Rolfe grew a crop. Once it was harvested, he invited friends to try smoking some of his tobacco. Their reaction was positive. Rolfe shipped the rest to England, where it proved extremely popular as well.

England also **imported** tobacco from Spain, which had a **monopoly** on the tobacco trade until 1617. Rolfe's experiment proved that the colonies could provide an equally good tobacco. This broke Spain's monopoly and marked the beginning of the early American tobacco industry.

In 1617, 20,000 pounds (9,072 kilograms) of tobacco leaf were **exported** from the colonies to England. In 1629, that figure rose to 1.5 million pounds (680,388 kg). For the next 64 years, tobacco was the most valuable major product shipped from the colonies.

THE MIDDLE COLONIES produced wheat, barley, oats, rye, and corn. In the southern colonies, most farmers grew tobacco. In South Carolina and Georgia, farmers grew rice and indigo, a plant whose berries were used to make a dark blue dye.

In 1614, John Rolfe married Pocahontas, daughter of Chief Powhatan. The marriage helped lessen conflicts between the Powhatan Indians and the colonists. After marrying, Pocahontas took the name Rebecca.

COLONIAL FARMS

Farming in the colonies was not an easy task. The soil in many areas was poor. Colonial farmers had no machinery. They relied on large numbers of people and animals to work the farms. Especially in the northeast, cold weather came early and lasted into late spring.

Servants and Slaves

In 1619, a Dutch **merchant** ship docked near Jamestown. The ship carried black people who had been taken by force. These people may have been from Africa but probably came from the West Indies, a chain of islands lying between Florida and Venezuela. Starving, the crew of the ship made a deal with the colonists to trade a group of the captives for food.

The captives on the Dutch ship became indentured servants. As such, they were forced to work in exchange for food and shelter. After a certain number of years, they would be set free. Usually, it took four to seven years for indentured servants to earn their freedom.

Until the mid-1660s, white indentured servants were common in North America. Mostly European, they made written agreements to work for someone in the colonies for a set period of time. In exchange, they often received passage to North America.

The flood of indentured servants into the colonies slowed as England's economic situation improved later in the 1600s. As pay rates rose and jobs became more plentiful, many workers chose to stay in their homeland.

1585–1640   1606–1616   1609–1629   1619   1620–1621   1629–1650

1650

A Stolen Dream

With fewer indentured servants available to work, American colonists looked elsewhere for help. Many planters in the South began to rely on black African labor.

In 1650, the colonies of Maryland and Virginia passed laws related to black and white indentured servants. The black servants were designated slaves, while the white servants were still able to earn their freedom.

This set the stage for white colonists to permanently own enslaved black people. For these previously indentured servants, freedom became a lost dream.

THE FIRST HISTORICAL evidence of the practice of slavery comes from a letter dated 1619. Within 80 years of that time, more than 20 percent of the people living in both Maryland and Virginia were enslaved workers.

1675–1676	1675–1676	1681–1683	1686–1713	1692–1693	1699–1751

Pilgrims at Plymouth

Many people came to North America to find religious freedom. The Pilgrims were a group who had completely separated from England's main religion, the Anglican Church of England. They did not believe in the church's practices and wanted to follow their own style of Christianity without fear of punishment. In the summer of 1620, the Pilgrims set sail for North America aboard the *Mayflower*. They landed at Plymouth Rock in today's Massachusetts on December 21, 1620.

That bitter winter, many of the Pilgrims lived on the *Mayflower*. During the day they worked onshore, building their settlement. At night, they retreated to the safety of the ship.

In March 1621, those who had survived the winter moved into the completed settlement. The Plymouth Colony settlers worked hard to build peaceful relations with neighboring American Indians. They learned how to hunt, fish, and grow crops. In the fall, after a successful harvest, the Pilgrims held a three-day feast with their neighbors. Grateful for their survival and all they had to eat, the colonists gave thanks. This first feast of celebration was the root of the American holiday of Thanksgiving.

THE PLYMOUTH COLONY settlers who arrived on the *Mayflower* referred to themselves as "Old Comers." However, in writing about Plymouth, colony leader William Bradford described the settlers as "pilgrims." Eventually, that name stuck.

1585–1640   1606–1616   1609–1629   1619–1650   1620   1629–1650

1621

FIRST THANKSGIVING

Little is known about the first Thanksgiving. One Pilgrim later wrote, "Amongst other recreations, we exercised our arms, many of the Indians coming amongst us, and among the rest, their greatest king Massasoit, with some ninety men . . ."

MAYFLOWER COMPACT

When the Pilgrims reached Plymouth Rock, the adult men signed a short written statement. This document is known as the Mayflower **Compact** because it was written on the ship. It was signed before the Pilgrims even touched land. According to the compact, dated November 11, 1620, all signers swore to be faithful to the English king. They also agreed to obey all colony laws made by their leaders, who were elected by majority vote.

WILLIAM BRADFORD

Bradford was one of the Plymouth Colony founders. He was also the author of the Mayflower Compact. Bradford was elected governor of Plymouth Colony in 1621, after the colony's first governor died. He served for 30 years.

The Great Puritan Migration

Following the **separatist** Pilgrims, another group migrated to North America around 1630. These people were known as Puritans because they felt the Church of England needed to be "purified" of its extravagant ways. The Puritan colonists had more interest in their religious lives than in seeking wealth. Most Puritans came to the new world in family groups rather than as single men or indentured servants. Nearly all of these colonists could read, and many were skilled artisans or craftsmen.

In 1629, the Massachusetts Bay Company was chartered by a group of Puritans. About 11,000 of them sailed to New England in 11 ships. The Puritans' goal was to set an example of pure and simple living for the rest of the world. Over the next 10 years, about 20,000 English people arrived to join the Massachusetts Bay colony.

Charles I became king of England in 1625. It was widely known that he hated the Puritans for criticizing the Anglican Church of England. Led by wealthy Puritan lawyer John Winthrop, those who joined the Massachusetts Bay colony had fled for their lives.

THE PURITANS' COLONY grew rapidly. By **1650**, the population was about 52,000. A little more than a century later, it would be close to 1.7 million.

Bacon's Rebellion

In July 1675, the Virginia colonists were becoming upset. Tobacco prices were going down, and the cost of goods was going up. This was especially true for goods made in England. Adding to the colonists' worries, severe weather had damaged crops and property.

When a group of local American Indians **raided** a Virginia plantation in July 1675, the colonists reacted with fear and anger. They struck back, but their attack went wrong. Fighting quickly worsened between the colonists and the American Indians. Virginia's governor, Sir William Berkeley, tried to please both sides. He wanted to stop the fighting, but it did not work.

A young, wealthy planter named Nathanial Bacon, Jr., rebelled. He thought Berkeley's government was **corrupt**. During the months of Bacon's Rebellion, Bacon and his men staged raids, openly **defied** Berkeley's orders, and drove the governor out of power. On September 19, 1676, Bacon burned most of Jamestown to ashes. He soon began losing the support of the people. Bacon died suddenly from an illness on October 26, 1676.

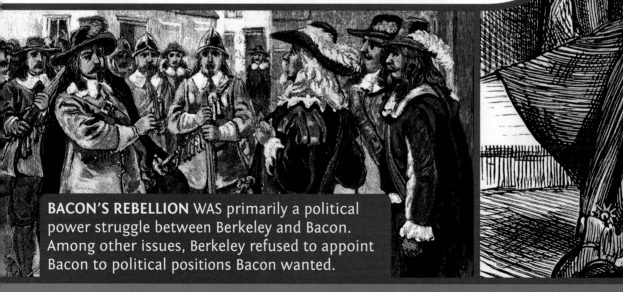

BACON'S REBELLION WAS primarily a political power struggle between Berkeley and Bacon. Among other issues, Berkeley refused to appoint Bacon to political positions Bacon wanted.

BACON'S GRIEVANCES

Bacon listed eight points that detailed the ways the English government had failed the colonists. First on his list was ". . . for not having, during this long time of his government, in any measure advanced this hopeful colony either by [forts for defense], towns, or trade."

WILLIAM BERKELEY

By 1676, Berkeley had been governor of Virginia for 30 years. He considered Bacon's rebellion a challenge to his own authority and accused Bacon of **treason**, a crime punishable by death. Berkeley later pardoned Bacon, but when he regained control as governor, he hanged 23 men for their part in Bacon's Rebellion.

DESPITE BEING ACCUSED of treason, Bacon had great political support. His supporters elected him into the Virginia government, and he attended a government assembly in June 1676.

1675

1676

1675–1676

1681–1683

1686–1713

1692–1693

1699–1751

17

King Philip's War

In the 1600s, the English rapidly settled throughout the area that came to be known as New England. The colonists' claims on the land caused increasing resentment among the region's American Indians. The American Indians had begun depending more and more on goods from the colonists. However, they were slowly being pushed off their lands. The settlers often took control by force.

In 1675, a Wampanoag chief named Metacom launched the last major American Indian effort to get rid of the colonists. Metacom, or "King Philip," as the English called him, led a series of attacks on settlement towns. Fierce battling continued into the spring of 1676. By early summer, the settlers had gained control. Metacom was killed on August 12, 1676, in Mount Hope, Rhode Island. This ended King Philip's War.

DURING KING PHILIP'S WAR, property was destroyed and countless people killed in violent attacks by both sides. Also known as Metacom's Rebellion, it was a costly conflict. Considered by percentages, the death rate in this war was twice as high as in the Civil War and seven times greater than in the American Revolution. For every ten who fought, both English and American Indian, one was wounded or killed. Most of these were American Indians.

Metacom, whose full name was Metacomet, was known for his pride and dignity. Two of Metacom's charges against the English were that American Indians were treated unequally in colonial courts and that the settlers' cattle destroyed his people's crops.

WHO WERE THE WAMPANOAG?

Wampanoag means "land where the Sun comes up first" or "People of the First Light." A large number of Wampanoag Indians had lived in southeastern New England for thousands of years by the time white Europeans arrived. From that point on, the Wampanoag population rapidly decreased. After King Philip's War, only 400 Wampanoag remained. Today, seven times that many Wampanoag live in this region, including on the islands of Nantucket and Martha's Vineyard.

Advertising for Colonists

In 1681, King Charles II granted Englishman William Penn an area of land along the Delaware River. There, Penn started a colony named Pennsylvania. In 1683, he wrote an advertisement to encourage Europeans to join the colony. It read, "The Air is Sweet and Clear, the Heavens Serene, like the South Parts of France." Penn also wrote letters to friends in England, hoping to interest them as well.

Penn, a Quaker, valued the principles of freedom and peace among people. These were Quaker values, but Penn had not been able to practice his religion freely in England. When he set up Pennsylvania's government, he created a list of privileges that would include these values. One of these was the freedom of worship. Penn also felt it was important to deal fairly with the local Delaware Indians. The Pennsylvania colony was successful in attracting settlers. In less than 20 years, Pennsylvania's population grew to 21,000.

1585–1640   1606–1616   1609–1629   1619–1650   1620–1621   1629–1650

Charting the Way to a New Colony

Early colonies were organized under one of three different types of charters. These were the Royal, Corporate, and Proprietary charters. Having a Royal charter meant the colony was controlled by the ruler who had granted the charter. A proprietary colony was owned by private landowners. Corporate charters were given to companies, such as the Virginia Company of England. That colony began under a charter from King James I, but the company hoped to make money from resources in North America.

WILLIAM PENN'S LAND grant covered parts of the modern-day states of Pennsylvania and Delaware. King Charles II gave William Penn the land to repay a debt he owed Penn's family.

1675–1676   1675–1676   1681   1686–1713   1692–1693   1699–1751

1683

Trouble from Across the Sea

By 1686, 12 of the original 13 American colonies had been established along the continent's east coast. They were Virginia, Massachusetts, New Hampshire, Maryland, Connecticut, Rhode Island, Delaware, North Carolina, South Carolina, New Jersey, New York, and Pennsylvania. Only Georgia was still to come, but not for another 46 years.

Unlike the colonizing efforts by Spain and France in other parts of the Americas, not all English colonies had been ordered by a **monarch**. By permission of the monarchy, a number of these colonies had been chartered by private parties with a stubborn will to succeed. Their goals were not always in line with England's greater goals.

All the colonies were affected by events in England, however. If someone new took over the throne or a war broke out, the American colonists were often affected. As the 1600s drew to a close, some of England's actions made particular impact in colonial America.

1686 DOMINION OF NEW ENGLAND

In 1686, English king James II began bringing the New England colonies together into a single **dominion**. Under the dominion's centralized control, the colonists lost their political rights and the power to govern themselves. Instead, King James appointed his own governors to oversee colonial affairs. This sowed seeds of rebellion throughout New England.

| 1585–1640 | 1606–1616 | 1609–1629 | 1619–1650 | 1620–1621 | 1629–1650 |

1688-1689 THE GLORIOUS REVOLUTION

In late 1688, King James II was overthrown. The English people were suspicious of the king's Roman Catholic leanings. In spring 1689, news of this so-called Glorious Revolution reached North America. New England's Catholic-hating Puritans rejoiced. In Boston, they arrested Sir Edmund Andros, the dominion's despised governor, as well others. The dominion dissolved, and the colonies returned to self-government. In England, James' daughter, Mary II, and her husband, William III of Orange, became the new rulers.

1689-1697 KING WILLIAM'S WAR

In Europe, King William II and his allies had launched the Nine Years' War against France in 1688. In 1689, the fighting spread to North America. The conflict there, known as King William's War, was a vicious struggle over land rights. It began with attacks on English settlements by French and American Indian forces. The English fought back, also with American Indian allies. The war ended in 1697, but neither side had gained control of the other.

1702 QUEEN ANNE'S WAR

In May 1702, England declared war on France under a new ruler, Queen Anne. As before, fighting erupted in North America as well. In this war, the English battled the French and Spanish in the northeast and as far south as Florida. American Indians joined both sides in fierce battles for land. Fighting ended in 1713 with no clear victor, but England had gained large parts of what today is eastern Canada. King William's War and Queen Anne's War were the first two parts of a longer conflict that became known as the French and Indian Wars.

1675–1676   1675–1676   1681–1683   1686   1692–1693   1699–1751

1713

Religion and Witchcraft

At the same time the English were fighting King William's War, another kind of conflict brewed in New England. This was the Puritans' war against witchcraft. Life in the New England colonies revolved around religion. The Puritans believed in strict punishment for those who did wrong. They also believed that evil, in the form of the Devil, could take power over people. According to the Puritans, the Devil often chose the weakest to do his work. They believed the Devil's helpers were witches. Anyone who practiced witchcraft was committing one of the worst sins possible.

The Puritans had come to North America to practice their religion freely. Now, as members of the Massachusetts Bay colony, they demanded that everyone follow their ways. Anyone who was "different" or did not go along with the Puritans' religious rules might be called a witch.

In February 1692, in the village of Salem, Massachusetts, two young cousins started behaving in strange and violent ways. A doctor declared that an "Evil Hand" was causing the girls' behavior. Soon, other teenage girls began behaving in the same ways. Panic spread through the colony. Several villagers were accused of being witches and causing the girls' troubles. During the Salem witch trials that followed, many innocent men and women were found guilty of witchcraft and hanged.

WOMEN AND WITCHCRAFT

The New England Puritans were suspicious of women who were different in some way, who freely expressed their opinions, or who lived alone. Not fitting well into the Puritans' strict, orderly society, such women were often the first to be accused of witchcraft. The Salem trials did not end until April 1693. During that time, more than 160 people were accused of witchcraft, and 19 were found guilty and hanged. Fourteen of those were women.

Cotton Mather was a powerful Puritan minister from Boston, Massachusetts. Mather called New England the "Devil's battlefield." He focused on the evils of witchcraft in his sermons and writings. Some historians believe Mather's intense focus on the Salem cases helped spread the fear that gripped the Puritans during the witch trials.

Troubled Times Ahead

In 1699, the English government passed the Wool Act. This was a law forbidding the colonies from exporting wool. This early restriction on colonial trade hinted at what was to come.

As the population of Colonial America grew and prospered, the English government tightened its control. In 1750, Great Britain's Iron Act put limits on colonial America's iron industry. In 1751, the Currency Act passed, making it illegal for the colonists to issue their own paper money.

By trial, error, and hard-won experience, these early settlers had come to feel at home in North America. They had farmed and built cities. They had put down roots and planned to stay. However, Great Britain did not want to give up its power over the colonies. The future was becoming clear. A fight for independence was looming in the colonists' future.

IN 1700, THE colonial population was slightly more than 250,000. Boston, the colonies' largest city, had just 7,000 residents. By 1750, however, the entire colonial population was more than 1 million. For many families, survival depended on farming successfully.

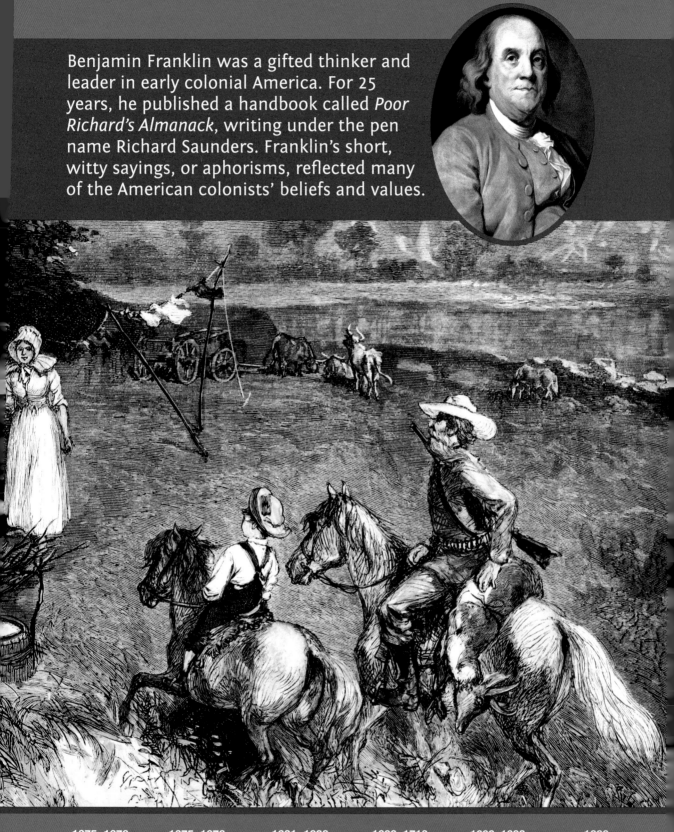

Benjamin Franklin was a gifted thinker and leader in early colonial America. For 25 years, he published a handbook called *Poor Richard's Almanack*, writing under the pen name Richard Saunders. Franklin's short, witty sayings, or aphorisms, reflected many of the American colonists' beliefs and values.

Activity

Fill in the Blanks

Timelines are only a beginning. They provide an overview of the key events and important people that shaped history. Now, research in the library and on the Internet to discover the rest of the story of how America was colonized.

Use a concept web to organize your ideas. Use the questions in the concept web to guide your research. When finished, use the completed web to help you write your report.

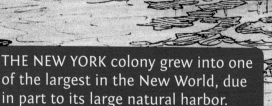

THE NEW YORK colony grew into one of the largest in the New World, due in part to its large natural harbor.

Concept Web

Important Events
- What significant events shaped the times or the person you are writing about?
- Were there any major events that triggered some turning point in the life or the time you are writing about?

Key People
- Discuss one or two main figures who had an impact on the times, event, or person you are researching.
- What negative or positive actions by people had a lasting effect on history?

Historic Places
- Discuss some of the most important places related to the subject of your research.
- Are there some important places that are not well-known today?
- If so, what are they and why were they important at the time or to your subject?

Causes
- How was your subject affected by important historical moments of the time?
- Was there any chain of events to cause a particular outcome in the event, time, or life you are researching?

Write a History Report

Obstacles
- What were some of the most difficult moments or events in the life of the person or in the historical timeline of the topic you are researching?
- Were there any particular people who greatly helped in overcoming obstacles?

Outcome and Lasting Effects
- What was the outcome of this chain of events?
- Was there a lasting effect on your subject?
- What is the importance of these "stepping stones" of history? How might the outcome have changed if things had happened differently?

Into the Future
- What lasting impact did your subject have on history?
- Is that person, time, or event well-known today?
- Have people's attitudes about your subject changed with the passage of time?
- Do people think differently today about the subject than they did at the time the event happened or the person was alive?

Brain Teaser

1. Who was the leader of the Pilgrims on the *Mayflower?*

2. What king set up the Dominion of New England?

3. The witch trials took place in which Massachusetts town?

4. Who married John Rolfe in 1614?

5. In what year did the Virginia Company settlers arrive in North America?

6. What did the English call Metacom?

7. Who started the rebellion against the Virginia colony's government?

8. The French and Indian War began with which two smaller wars?

9. What was the most valuable export for the colonies?

10. Who is the state of Pennsylvania named after?

11. How many Puritans sailed to New England in the Great Puritan Migration?

12. Which three types of charters were the original colonies organized under?

12. a royal charter, a corporate charter, or a proprietary charter
11. 11,000
10. William Penn
9. Tobacco
8. Queen Anne's War and King William's War
7. Nathaniel Bacon, Jr.
6. King Philip
5. 1607
4. Pocahontas
3. Salem
2. King James II
1. William Bradford

ANSWERS

Key Words

charter: formal document that creates an institution such as a company

colonizing: sending groups of people to new places in order to create colonies, or settlements, there

colony: a territory that has been settled and is ruled by a distant country

compact: a formal agreement between two or more parties

corrupt: not following the proper rules or laws of how a government should be run

defied: went against

dominion: a country or territory under the control of another nation

expansion: the act of growing larger

exported: sent to another country

imported: brought in from another country

income: money received or earned

merchant: a person or company that sells or trades goods

monarch: head of a country; usually a king or queen

monopoly: the complete possession or control of the supply of a product:

raided: attacked suddenly without warning

separatist: someone who separates, or breaks away, from an established group

settlement: a newly colonized area

timber: wood that has been prepared for use in construction or carpentry

treason: actions that go against a person's own country

Index

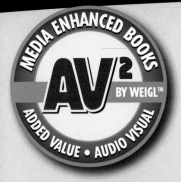

Log on to www.av2books.com

AV² by Weigl brings you media enhanced books that support active learning. Go to www.av2books.com, and enter the special code found on page 2 of this book. You will gain access to enriched and enhanced content that supplements and complements this book. Content includes video, audio, weblinks, quizzes, a slide show, and activities.

AV² Online Navigation

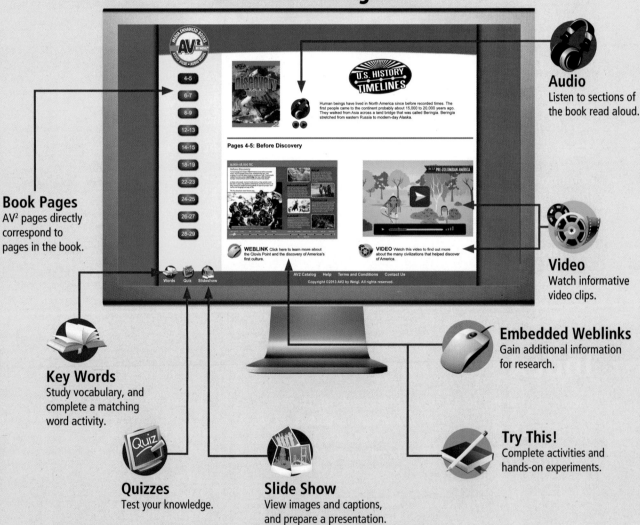

Audio
Listen to sections of the book read aloud.

Book Pages
AV² pages directly correspond to pages in the book.

Video
Watch informative video clips.

Embedded Weblinks
Gain additional information for research.

Key Words
Study vocabulary, and complete a matching word activity.

Try This!
Complete activities and hands-on experiments.

Quizzes
Test your knowledge.

Slide Show
View images and captions, and prepare a presentation.

AV² was built to bridge the gap between print and digital. We encourage you to tell us what you like and what you want to see in the future.

Sign up to be an AV² Ambassador at www.av2books.com/ambassador.

Due to the dynamic nature of the Internet, some of the URLs and activities provided as part of AV² by Weigl may have changed or ceased to exist. AV² by Weigl accepts no responsibility for any such changes. All media enhanced books are regularly monitored to update addresses and sites in a timely manner. Contact AV² by Weigl at 1-866-649-3445 or av2books@weigl.com with any questions, comments, or feedback.